FlyHigh
Activity Book

3

Jeanne Perrett   Charlotte Covill
with Tamzin Thompson

T0345696

Contents

⓵ He's from Africa.

① Circle the family words.

(mum) holiday grandma Africa cousin elephant zoo brother sister

airport uncle zebra aunt mobile phone grandpa Spain dad friend

② Write. Use family words from Exercise 1.

1 This is my mum. This is her sister.
She's my _____aunt_____ .

2 This is my aunt. This is her baby boy.
He's my _____ .

3 This is my dad. This is his brother.
He's my _____ .

③ Write am, is or are.

My name (**1**) ____is____ Trumpet. I (**2**) _____
an elephant. Ziggy (**3**) _____ a zebra. He
(**4**) _____ from Africa. We (**5**) _____ friends.
He (**6**) _____ in England on holiday. His aunt,
uncle and cousin (**7**) _____ here too. I
(**8**) _____ very happy.

4 Choose and write. Then colour.

India ~~Australia~~ Africa

~~red~~ / white / blue   orange / white / green   black / red / green

1 Karla ....is from Australia.... . Her flag is ......red............ , ...
and ....

2 Ziggy .... His flag is .... , ...
and ....

3 Tag .... His .... , ...
and ....

5 Match.

1 Hello. How are you?   **a** My name is Sarah.

2 What's your name?   **b** I'm fine, thank you.

3 Where are you from?   **c** It's red, white and blue.

4 What colour is your flag?   **d** I'm from England.

6 Look at Exercise 5. Write. Then answer about you.

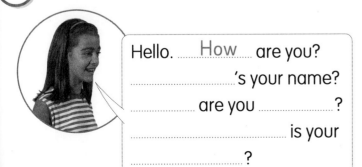

Hello. ......How...... are you?
.....................'s your name?
.... are you .... ?
.... is your
.... ?

I'm ...., thank you.
My ....
I'm ....
It's ....

(2) Are you on holiday?

(1) Choose and write.

 (shy) / tired   happy / hungry   cheese / spaghetti   tall / short

1 He's ...shy... .   **2** She's ....   **3** It's ....   **4** They're ....

(2) Correct the sentences.

1 Ziggy is from England.
He ...isn't... from England. ...He's... from Africa.

2 His cousin is shy.
She .... shy. .... tired.

3 His aunt and uncle are elephants.
They .... elephants. .... zebras.

4 You're twelve years old.
I .... twelve years old. .... years old.

5 We're on holiday.
We .... on holiday. .... at school.

6 I'm tall.
You .... tall. .... short.

(3) Match.

1 Is your name Ziggy?   **a** Yes, we are.
2 Are you from England?   **b** No, she isn't.
3 Are you and your family on holiday?   **c** No, I'm not.
4 Are your mum and dad here?   **d** Yes, he is.
5 Is your cousin shy?   **e** Yes, it is.
6 Is Trumpet your friend?   **f** No, they aren't.

4 Write Are or Is. Look and answer.

1 Is he a policeman?   Yes, he is.   **4** _____ she a dancer?   ....
2 Are they kangaroos?   No, they're tigers.   **5** _____ they bears?   ....
3 _____ she a firefighter?   ....   **6** _____ it a doll?   ....

5 Write questions. Then answer.

1 Sam / Australia?
    Is Sam from Australia?   Yes, he is.

2 Natalia / Russia?
    Is Natalia from Russia?   No,

3 Ivan / Turkey?
    ....

4 Carlos and Pedro / Ukraine?
    ....

5 John and Sally / Britain?
    ....

VISITORS BOOK

Name	Country
John	Britain
Natalia	Ukraine
Carlos	Argentina
Sally	Britain
Pedro	Argentina
Ivan	Russia
Sam	Australia

6 Write the questions in the correct order. Then answer about you.

1 years / Are / ten / you / old?
    Are you ten years old?   ....

2 Is / hair / your / long?
    ....

3 eyes / green? / Are / your
    ....

4 a dancer? / mum / Is / your
    ....

3 I've got a camera.

1 Match. Write the names.

John   Fred   Paul   Nick

1   He's got a flag, an ice cream and sunglasses.   ...Fred...
2   They've got ice creams.   .... and ....
3   He's got a map, sunglasses and a flag.   ....
4   They've got maps.   .... and ....
5   He's got a camera, a flag and sunglasses.   ....
6   They've got cameras.   .... and ....

2 Read and colour.

She's got a yellow sun hat.
She's got brown hair.
She's got a red and orange shirt.
She's got green and blue shorts.
She's got a pink and white swimsuit.
She's got purple shoes.

3 Draw, colour and write about you.

I've got lots of clothes for my holiday.
I've got .... shorts.
I've got a .... T-shirt.
I've got a .... sweater.
I've got .... sunglasses.

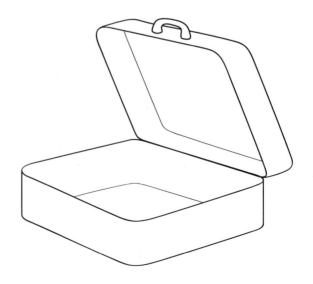

4 **Look, choose and write. Use** have got **or** has got.

Mr Brown | Mrs Brown | George | Polly | Jane | Vicky

Sally | Tom | Emma | Peter | Rob | Harry

1 Mr and Mrs Brown ____have got books____ . **5** Emma _____ .

2 Sally _____ . **6** Polly and Jane _____ .

3 George _____ . **7** Vicky _____ .

4 Tom and Peter _____ . **8** Harry and Rob _____ .

5 **Write.**

Long forms	Short forms

Long forms

1 I ____have got____ brown eyes.

2 You _____ lots of clothes.

3 He _____ a camera.

4 She _____ sunglasses.

5 We _____ new bikes.

6 They _____ rollerblades.

Short forms

1 I ____'ve got____ brown eyes.

2 You _____ lots of clothes.

3 He _____ a camera.

4 She _____ sunglasses.

5 We _____ new bikes.

6 They _____ rollerblades.

Look!

Tom <u>has got</u> a map. **He** <u>'s got</u> a map.
Tom and Peter <u>have got</u> a ball. **They** <u>'ve got</u> a ball

6 **Write about you. Use** 've got**,** have got **or** has got.

1 I _____ eyes.

2 My friend, _____, _____ a pet _____ .

3 My cousin, _____, _____ hair.

4 My grandma and grandpa _____ a big _____ .

9

4 Have you got your passports?

1 Look, read and circle.

1 He 's got / hasn't got a passport.
2 He 's got / hasn't got a map.
3 He 's got / hasn't got a ticket.
4 He 's got / hasn't got a suitcase.
5 He 's got / hasn't got sunglasses.
6 He 's got / hasn't got a mobile phone.
7 He 's got / hasn't got a camera.
8 He 's got / hasn't got a hat.

2 Look and write. Use have/haven't got or has/hasn't got.

	📷	✈️	🐕	⌚
Rob	✔	✔	✗	✔
Sally	✗	✔	✔	✔
Mary and Sue	✔	✗	✔	✔
You				

1 Rob ....has got a camera, a toy plane.... and a ....
   He ....hasn't got a.... ....
2 Sally ....
   She ....
3 Mary and Sue ....
   They ....

Complete the table and write about you. Use I've got **or** I haven't got.

....

....

3 **Look at Exercise 2. Write** Have **or** Has**. Then circle.**

1   Has .... Rob got a camera?   (Yes, he has.)/ No, he hasn't.
2   .... Sally got a watch?   Yes, she has. / No, she hasn't.
3   .... Mary and Sue got toy planes?   Yes, they have. / No, they haven't.
4   .... you got a dog?   Yes, I have. / No, I haven't.

4 **Write the questions in the correct order. Then answer.**

1   the cat / a ball? / got / Has
    Has the cat got a ball?   Yes, it has.
2   Have / suitcases? / got / the ducks
    ....
3   got / the horse / Has / a suitcase?
    ....
4   the boy / Has / got / a passport?
    ....
5   a map? / got / Have / the girls
    ....

5 **Write questions. Then answer about you.**

1   you / a passport?   Have you got   ?   ....
2   your dad / a car?   ....
3   your friends / computers?   ....
4   your grandma / a mobile phone?   ....

11

Sally's Story
Snowy

1   **Read and circle.**

1   Joanna has got her Maths book.

(yes) / no

2   Joanna has got her History book.

yes / no

3   Joanne has got her English book.

yes / no

4   Joanna has got her Art book.

yes / no

2   **Put the letters in the correct order. Write the words.**

What day is it today?

1   y n M d o a   It's ___Monday___.

2   d y F i r a   It's _____.

3   a n u y S d   It's _____.

4   a s u T y d e   It's _____.

5   u a t y S a r d   It's _____.

6   y T a d s u r h   It's _____.

7   e n y W d a s e d   It's _____.

3 Write questions. Then answer.

1 Art / Monday?
   Has he got Art on Monday?   Yes, he has.

2 English / Tuesday?
   ....

3 PE / Wednesday?
   ....

4 History / Thursday?
   ....

5 Maths / Friday?
   ....

4 Look at Exercise 3 and write.

On Monday, I've got Art , ... and ....
I .... PE.

What about you?

5 Complete the timetable for you. Then write.

Monday	Tuesday	Wednesday	Thursday	Friday

On Monday I've got .... , ... and ....
I haven't got ....
On ....
....
....
....
....
....
....

13

1 Write the words in the correct box.

~~shorts~~ PE plane
sunglasses shirt
ticket Art suitcase
History passport
Maths swimsuit

Clothes	School	Holidays
shorts		

2 Look and write.

John   Kelly Ted   Jenny Carol   Ron   Alex

My name is Ted. I've got a (1) ......sister...... . Her name is (2) ....
I've got a (3) .... Her name is Jenny. I've got a dad. His name is
(4) .... (5) .... an aunt. (6) .... Carol.
I've got an (7) .... His name is Ron. (8) .... a cousin.
His name is (9) ....

3 Match.

1 Has Kate got a bike?   a Yes, I have.
2 Have you got a cat?   b No, we haven't.
3 Has James got a rabbit?   c Yes, it has.
4 Have your cousins got watches? d No, he hasn't.
5 Have you and Mark got passports? e Yes, she has.
6 Has your dog got a ball?   f No, they haven't.

4 Write questions. Then answer.

1 they / tickets? <u>Have they got tickets?</u>   Yes, they have.

2 she / a sandwich? <u>Has she got a sandwich?</u>   No, she hasn't. She's got an ice cream.

3 she / a mobile phone? ....

4 it / a map? ....

5 she / sunglasses? ....

6 she / an ice cream? ....

7 he / a passport? ....

My English

Read and colour.

1 Is she your sister? Yes, she is. / No, she isn't.

2 Are you shy? Yes, I am. / No, I'm not.

3 Have you got a camera? Yes, I have. / No, I haven't.

4 Has your brother got a dog? Yes, he has. / No, he hasn't.

5 The postman comes at seven.

1 Choose and write.

afternoon   night   ~~morning~~   evening

1 _morning_   **2** _____   **3** _____   **4** _____

2 Match.

a    b

1 It's three o'clock.
2 It's four o'clock.
3 It's eleven o'clock.
4 It's one o'clock.
5 It's seven o'clock.
6 It's nine o'clock.

d    e

c

f

3 Put the letters in the correct order. Choose and write.

1 tanomps   **2** crepal   **3** telert   **4** radocpts

1 The _____postman_____ comes every morning.
2 I've got a _____. It's big! What is it?
3 We've got a _____ from grandma. It's very long!
4 It's a _____ from my friend. There's a picture of France on it.

4 **Write the correct forms.**

do

1   I ....do.... my homework in my bedroom.
2   My brother ....does.... his homework in the kitchen.

play

3   I .... the violin.
4   My brother .... the guitar.

go

5   I .... to the park on Saturdays.
6   My brother .... to the swimming pool on Saturdays.

watch

7   I .... dancers on TV.
8   My brother .... football on TV.

5 **Choose and write. Use the correct forms.**

1 In the morning Harry and Katie ....go to town.....
2 In the afternoon they .... He .... and she
   ....
3 In the evening he .... and she ....

6 **Write.**

Hello from sunny France. Every morning we
(**1**) ....go.... (go) to the beach. My mum
(**2**) .... (swim) in the sea and I
(**3**) .... (play) football with my dad. My
baby sister (**4**) .... (play) on the beach.
We (**5**) .... (eat) ice-cream too. In the
afternoon we (**6**) .... (go) to town.
In the evening my sister (**7**) .... (go)
to bed at seven o'clock. Then mum and dad
(**8**) .... (watch) TV and I
(**9**) .... (write) postcards.

Sam Smith
19 Forest Road
Manchester

6 Do they play basketball?

1 Find, circle and tick.

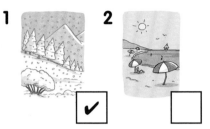

w	z	s	u	m	m	e	r	t
e	y	a	g	h	e	t	t	y
e	y	t	s	k	i	l	p	e
k	r	r	w	u	p	s	e	a
e	e	k	t	s	e	b	d	r
n	c	w	i	n	t	e	r	m
d	r	y	b	t	q	s	n	g
m	o	u	n	t	a	i	n	s

2 Read and write. Use words from Exercise 1.

1 We swim in the sea in ....summer.......... .

2 He wears a warm sweater in ....

3 They .... every afternoon.

4 We go to the .... every summer.

5 I play basketball every ....

6 We go to the beach every ....

3 Read and circle for you.

1 I ski / don't ski in winter.

2 I watch / don't watch TV in the afternoon.

3 I play / don't play computer games in the evening.

4 My friends and I play / don't play football at the weekend.

5 I do / don't do my homework on Sunday.

4 **Write. Use** don't.

1 My family and I go to the park at the weekend. _We don't go_ to the beach.

2 My sisters climb on the climbing frame. .... trees.

3 My cousin and I play football. .... basketball.

4 I wear a T-shirt in summer. .... a sweater.

5 My mum and dad read books. .... postcards.

6 We eat ice creams. .... pizza.

5 **Write. Then circle.**

Friday   Sunday   Tuesday   Saturday

1 ...Do... your mum and dad buy pizza on Friday?   (Yes, they do.)/ No, they don't.

2 .... your mum and dad watch TV on Sunday?   Yes, they do. / No, they don't.

3 .... you play football with your friends on Tuesday?   Yes, I do. / No, I don't.

4 .... you learn Maths on Tuesday?   Yes, I do. / No, I don't.

5 .... you and your sister go to school at the weekend?   Yes, we do. / No, we don't.

6 .... you play with trains on Saturday?   Yes, I do. / No, I don't.

6 **Write the questions in the correct order. Then answer about you.**

1 homework / do / on Saturday? / you / Do / your
Do you do your homework on Saturday? ....

2 your friends / every winter? / Do / ski
....

3 watch TV / Do / in the evening? / you and your friends
....

4 Do / read / every day? / you
....

5 at seven o'clock? / get up / Do / your mum and dad
....

6 you and your family / every year? / Do / on holiday / go
....

7 She doesn't like meat.

1 Circle.

1
England
(China)
Turkey

2
leaf
flower
tree

3
spaghetti
meat
cheese

4
Ukraine
Argentina
Africa

5
penguin
zebra
panda

6
shy
excited
tired

2 Choose and write.

sleeps   meat   leaves   panda   China   ~~excited~~

Everyone at the zoo is (**1**) ....excited........ There's a new animal at the zoo. Pandora is a (**2**) .... She comes from (**3**) .... She eats (**4**) .... She doesn't like (**5**) .... She (**6**) .... a lot!

3 Read and correct the sentences.

Trumpet comes from China.
He eats meat.
He lives in the jungle.
He wears a blue hat.

Comes from:	Africa
Eats:	leaves
Lives:	zoo
Wears:	a green hat

Trumpet doesn't come from China. He comes from Africa.
He

4 Look at Exercise 3. Read and circle.

1 Does Trumpet live in the jungle?   Yes, he does. / No, he doesn't.
2 Does he eat leaves?   Yes, he does. / No, he doesn't.
3 Does he wear a blue hat?   Yes, he does. / No, he doesn't.
4 Does he come from Africa?   Yes, he does. / No, he doesn't.
5 Does he eat meat?   Yes, he does. / No, he doesn't.
6 Does he live in the zoo?   Yes, he does. / No, he doesn't.

5 Look and write.

Tom	✔	✗	✔	✔
Sue	✗	✗	✔	✗
You				

1 Does Sue play football?
    No, she doesn't.

4 Does Sue eat meat?
    ....

2 Does Tom eat meat?
    ....

5 Does Tom play football?
    ....

3 Do Tom and Sue ski?
    ....

6 Do Tom and Sue swim?
    ....

Complete the table and write about you.

....

....

6 Write Do or Does. Then answer about you.

1 __Does__ your teacher wear black shoes?   ....
2 .... your friends like basketball?   ....
3 .... your mum eat fish?   ....
4 .... you rollerblade?   ....
5 .... your dad play basketball?   ....
6 .... your friends watch TV every day?   ....

8 They always wake up early.

1 What's missing? Look and match. Then draw.

1	2	3	4	5	6
early	want	wake up	late	bird	show

2 Read and write. Use words from Exercise 1.

1 On Sunday Patty _shows_ Pandora the zoo.

2 We live next to the ....

3 We .... early.

4 We never wake up ....

5 I .... a shower, too!

3 Answer about you.

1 Do you wake up early every day? ....

2 Do you go to bed late at the weekend? ....

3 Do you like birds? ....

4 Do you show your homework to your mum? ....

5 What do you want for your birthday? ....

4 **Look and write. Use ● always, ◐ sometimes or ○ never.**

1 She _sometimes has_ (have) a shower in the morning.

2 She _____ (eat) breakfast.

3 She _____ (walk) to school.

4 She _____ (get up) early.

5 **Write about you. Use always, sometimes or never and the correct verb form.**

1 I _____ (help) at home at the weekend.

2 I _____ (ride) my bike to school.

3 My dad _____ (sing) in the shower.

4 My friends and I _____ (play) football after school.

5 I _____ (take) photos on holiday.

6 We _____ (play) computer games at school.

7 I _____ (get up) late on Sunday.

8 My English teacher _____ (wear) a red sweater.

6 **Write the words in the correct order. Then tick (✓) or cross (✗) for you.**

1 always / get up / on Sunday. / early / I

   I always get up early on Sunday. _____

2 meat. / eats / never / teacher / Our

   _____

3 the evening. / TV / I / watch / sometimes / in

   _____

4 always / school. / walk / We / to

   _____

5 My / shoes. / wears / friend / sometimes / brown

   _____

6 always / on holiday / go / We / in summer.

   _____

The months of the year

1 **Choose and write. Then match.**

summer   autumn   spring   ~~winter~~

 **a**  **b**  **c**  **d** 1

1 The ___winter___ trees are black and brown.

2 _____ is the time to play.

3 Yellow leaves fall from the _____ trees.

4 The birds are happy now it's _____ .

2 **Put the letters in the correct order. Write the words in the correct place.**

cebreDem   neuJ   yuFarerb   arJnayu   yMa   pebtermSe

ervNmobe   gAsutu   hacMr   lJyu   piAlr   ecorbOt

Spring	**Summer**	**Autumn**	**Winter**
....	....	....	....
....	....	....	....
....	....	....	....

3 **Match and write.**

1 In spring   families   fall from the trees.
2 In summer   children   go to the beach.
3 In autumn   birds   make snowmen.
4 In winter   leaves   make nests.

1 ___In spring birds make nests.___   **3** _____

2 _____   **4** _____

24

4 **Choose, circle and write.**

1 In spring we can ....see baby animals.... and ....
   (a) see baby animals   **b** play in the leaves   **c** hear the birds
2 In summer we can .... and ....
   a swim in the sea   **b** go on holiday   **c** ski in the mountains
3 In autumn we can .... and ....
   a go to school again   **b** fly our kites   **c** play in the snow
4 In winter we can .... and ....
   a wear warm sweaters   **b** see lots of flowers   **c** have a New Year party

5 **Choose and write.**

~~play~~   beach   fly   leaves   animals   sea   snow   see   sweater

In spring I **(1)** ....play.... outside in the sunshine every day. I **(2)** .... lots of flowers and I sometimes see baby **(3)** .... too.
In summer I always go to the **(4)** .... with my family and I swim in the **(5)** ....
In autumn I sometimes **(6)** .... my kite at the weekend and I sometimes play in the **(7)** ....
In winter I always play in the **(8)** .... and I always wear a warm **(9)** .... and a hat.

What about you?

6 **Write about what you do in spring, summer, autumn and winter. Use ideas from Exercise 4 and Exercise 5. Stick a photo.**

In spring I ....
In summer ....
In ....
....
....

The FlyHigh Review 2

1 Write.

Months → M Seasons → S Animals → A Time of day → T

panda _____A_____   autumn _____   January _____   tiger _____
September _____   evening _____   spring _____   morning _____
night _____   bird _____   zebra _____   July _____
summer _____   February _____   afternoon _____   winter _____

2 Look, choose and write the correct verb forms.

visit ~~play~~ ride have watch do read go swim

	Monday	Tuesday	Wednesday	Thursday	Friday	Saturday and Sunday

On Monday Vicky (1) _____plays_____ tennis after school. Rob (2) _doesn't play_ tennis. He (3) _____ football.

On Tuesday Vicky (4) _____ a guitar lesson in the evening. Rob (5) _____ a guitar lesson. He (6) _____ TV.

On Wednesday Vicky (7) _____ a book in her bedroom. Rob (8) _____ a book. He (9) _____ his bike to the playground.

On Thursday Vicky (10) _____ at the pool. Rob (11) _____ at the pool too.

On Friday Vicky (12) _____ her homework. Rob (13) _____ his homework. He (14) _____ a friend.

At the weekend they (15) _____ to the zoo. They (16) _____ to the park.

3 **Look at Exercise 2. Write Do or Does. Then answer.**

1 _Does_ Vicky play tennis on Monday? _Yes, she does._
2 .... Rob have a guitar lesson on Tuesday? ....
3 .... Vicky go to the playground on Wednesday? ....
4 .... Rob and Vicky swim on Thursday? ....
5 .... Rob do his homework on Friday? ....
6 .... Rob and Vicky go to the zoo at the weekend? ....

4 **Read and write the names.**

1 _Susan_   2 ....   3 ....   4 ....   5 ....   6 ....

Susan and Jenny are sisters. Susan always gets up early. She sometimes has a shower in the morning. She always has egg and toast for breakfast. She never walks to school. She sometimes plays games in the playground before school.

Jenny never gets up early. She never has a shower in the morning. She always has bread and honey for breakfast. She always walks to school. She sometimes talks to friends in the playground before school.

5 **Choose and write about you. Use always, sometimes or never.**

swim   do my homework   play football   visit my friend   watch TV

1 ....   3 ....
2 ....   4 ....

My English

Read and colour.

1   We get up at 8 o'clock.

2   Do you ski in winter? Yes, I do. / No, I don't.

3   Does your mum make cakes? Yes, she does. / No, she doesn't.

4   I often play basketball on Saturday.

FUN TIME 1

1 Find and circle. Then say.

1　k

2　g

3　j

4　x

2 Put the letters in the correct order. Write the words in the correct box.

~~nkig~~　angoorak　jllye　egma　itxa　pujm　rlgi　xsi

k	g	j	x
king			

3 Circle and write. Then find the secret word.

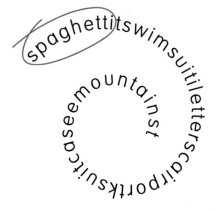

1　We eat this for dinner.　　spaghetti
2　We ski here.
3　We put clothes in this.
4　We can see planes here.
5　We wear this in the sea.
6　We write these to our friends.

The secret word is: ....

4 **Read, match and answer.**

1 Peter has got a suitcase.

2 Daisy has got sunglasses.

3 Paul has got the passports.

4 Anna has got a book.

5 Jim has got a mobile phone.

6 Jane has got a bag.

7 Sam has got a computer game.

What has Mary got? ....

5 **Do the crossword and answer the question.**

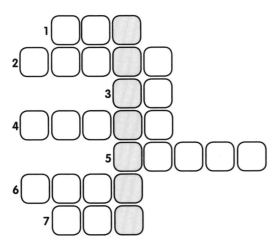

1 I haven't .... a passport.

2 They walk to school .... day.

3 We get .... early on Monday.

4 He .... in the pool in summer.

5 My friend sometimes .... the guitar.

6 .... you got a brother?

7 'Do pandas .... leaves?' 'Yes, they do.'

Who has got a friend in Africa? ....

9 I'm cooking.

1 Do the crossword. Write.

 1

 2

 3

 4

 5

 6

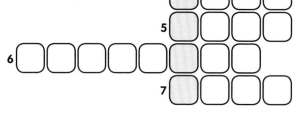

 7

The secret word is ....

2 Write and match. Use 'm, 're or 's.

1 I ....'m.... learning
2 You .... cleaning
3 He .... talking
4 She .... cooking
5 We .... ringing
6 They .... walking

a the doorbell.
b spaghetti.
c home from school.
d the kitchen.
e a new song.
f to his friends.

3 Look, choose and write. Use 'm, 're or 's.

writing   singing   eating   sleeping   ~~reading~~   making

1 She 's reading ....

2 We .... a cake.

3 I ....

4 They ....

5 He ....

6 It ....

4 Read and write the correct form.

In the classroom …

1 We _'re learning_ (learn) English today.
2 We _____ (listen) to the teacher.
3 The teacher _____ (write) on the board.
4 I _____ (read) my English book.
5 The school bell _____ (ring).
6 Our teacher _____ (say) 'Goodbye'.
7 We _____ (go) to the playground.

5 Choose and write the correct form.

do a handstand   ~~fly~~   play football
have fun   watch the girl   climb a tree

1 The ducks _are flying_ .
2 The cat _____ .
3 The girl _____ .
4 The dog _____ .
5 The boys _____ .
6 They _____ .

6 Read, choose and write the correct form.

take   climb   ~~shine~~   ride   have   listen
sleep   write   play

It's Sunday. My family and I are in the park. My friends are
here too. (**1**) The sun _is shining_ . (**2**) My
cousins _____ football.
(**3**) My sister _____ her new bike and (**4**) my
brother _____ a tree. The baby is very quiet –
(**5**) she _____ .
(**6**) My mum and dad _____ to the radio.
(**7**) My grandma _____ a letter. (**8**) My friend and
I _____ photos. (**9**) We _____ lots of fun.

(10) You aren't helping.

(1) Put the letters in the correct order. Choose and write.

ahsw   satet   sidh   ~~akem~~   werybrsart   oforl

1 _make_   **2** _____   **3** _____   **4** _____   **5** _____   **6** _____

(2) Find the differences. Choose and write the correct form.

make   ~~wash~~   clean   taste

In Picture A …	In Picture B …
1 The girl _is washing_ the dishes.	She _isn't washing_ the dishes.
2 The boy _____ a strawberry.	He _____ a strawberry.
3 The woman _____ a cake.	She _____ a cake.
4 The man _____ the floor.	He _____ the floor.

(3) Choose and write negative sentences.

play   ~~wear~~   sleep   listen   do   watch

1 Tom _isn't wearing_ a sweater today. It's hot.

2 The cat _____. It's playing in the garden.

3 Sally _____ TV. She's eating lunch.

4 Rob and Vicky _____ to the radio. They're talking to Sally.

5 We _____ basketball. We're reading.

6 The children _____ their homework. They're making a cake.

4 Look and write.

1 play with her toys / sleep
The baby ___isn't playing with her toys___ . She ___'s sleeping___ .

2 have breakfast / do his homework
The boy _____ . He _____ .

3 cook lunch / eat lunch
The girl _____ . She _____ .

4 fly kites / watch TV
The boys _____ . They _____ .

5 Read and write the correct form.

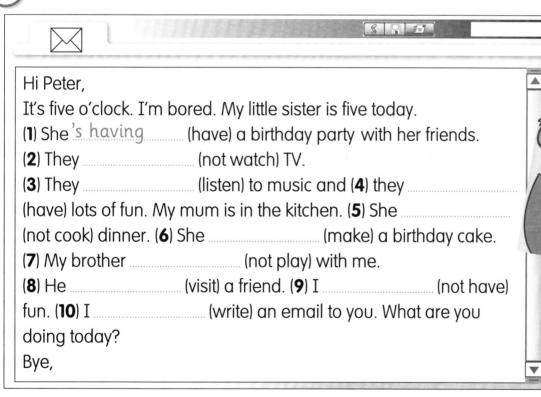

Hi Peter,
It's five o'clock. I'm bored. My little sister is five today.
(**1**) She ___'s having___ (have) a birthday party with her friends.
(**2**) They _____ (not watch) TV.
(**3**) They _____ (listen) to music and (**4**) they _____
(have) lots of fun. My mum is in the kitchen. (**5**) She _____
(not cook) dinner. (**6**) She _____ (make) a birthday cake.
(**7**) My brother _____ (not play) with me.
(**8**) He _____ (visit) a friend. (**9**) I _____ (not have)
fun. (**10**) I _____ (write) an email to you. What are you
doing today?
Bye,

6 Write about you.

1 learn English   ___I'm learning English.___

2 wear black shoes   _____

3 have a shower   _____

4 write an exercise   _____

5 do my homework

11 Are you going to town?

1 **Choose and write. Then match.**

~~buy~~   go   read   climb   walk   carry   watch

library   rope   ~~supermarket~~   airport   cinema   school

1 She 's buying food.
She's in the supermarket .

2 He .... a book.
He's in the ....

3 She .... a film.
She's in the ....

4 She .... a mountain.
She's got a ....

5 They .... suitcases.
They're at the ....

6 They ....
They're .... to
....

a

b

c

1

d

e

f

2 **Write Am, Is or Are. Then match.**

1 Am I wearing black shoes?   **a** Yes, she is.
2 .... we going to the cinema?   **b** Yes, you are.
3 .... they buying tickets?   **c** No, I'm not.
4 .... he making a cake?   **d** Yes, we are.
5 .... you taking a photo?   **e** No, he isn't.
6 .... she carrying a suitcase?   **f** No, they aren't.

3 Write the questions and answer.

1 the woman / buy / apples?

Is the woman buying apples?　　　　No, she isn't. She's buying bananas.

2 the girls / laugh?

....　　..

3 the man / carry / a suitcase?

....　　..

4 the boy / play / with the girls?

....　　..

5 the dog / jump?

....　　..

4 Write the questions in the correct order. Then answer about you.

1 T-shirt? / you / a / wearing / Are

Are you wearing a T-shirt?　　　　..

2 it / raining? / Is

....　　..

3 to / Are / your / going / the cinema? / friends

....　　..

4 your / dishes? / the / dad / Is / washing

....　　..

5 you / TV? / Are / watching

....　　..

6 Is / cooking / mum / spaghetti? / your

....　　..

12 Wait here. Don't move.

1 Circle and write.

wait / (stop)

1 You're making a mess. Please ....stop........ .

run / wait

2 We .... for the bus every morning.

postman / thief

3 Help! A .... is taking our things!

chase / wash

4 My dog likes to .... cats.

brave / bored

5 The police are very ....

move / make

6 Don't .... please. I'm taking your photo.

2 Look, choose and write.

Let's ride our bikes.   Let's have an apple.   Let's go to the library.   Let's go shopping.

1 ....

2 ....

3 ....

3 Match.

1 I'm hungry.
2 It's cold today.
3 The baby is sleeping.
4 What a mess!
5 You're tired.
6 It's time for school.

a Go to bed.
b Don't be late.
c Let's clean the kitchen.
d Wear your sweater.
e Don't make a noise.
f Let's make a pizza.

4 Look, choose and write.

Let's move.   Don't move.   ~~Move!~~

Don't sit down.   Let's sit down.   Sit down, please!

1 .... Move!

2 ....

3 ....

4 ....

5 ....

6 ....

5 Read and write. Use Let's or Don't.

1 It's a beautiful day. ...Let's... go for a walk.
2 You're wearing your new shoes. Please .... climb the tree.
3 It's time for lunch. .... cook spaghetti.
4 .... play football in the classroom.
5 Stop! .... go. A car is coming!
6 This is a library. .... talk, please.
7 It's my birthday. .... make a cake.

The bear fight

1 Read and tick (✓) or cross (✗).

1 Grandma is playing. ....✗........

Adam is swinging on a rope. ......✓......

2 The boys are climbing a mountain. ....

The boys are sleeping. ....

3 Grandma is chasing the bear. ....

The boys are fighting the bear. ....

4 The boys are playing a computer game. ....

There's a bear in the bedroom. ....

2 Add -ing and write in the correct box.

~~run~~   ~~climb~~   ~~have~~   sit   ride   shine   make   ski   play   sleep   skip   swim

+ -ing	~~e~~+ -ing	double letter + -ing
climbing	having	running

3 Read and write the correct form.

A I'm at the park. (**1**) It's sunny but the wind ....is blowing.... (blow). (**2**) My friend .... (ride) a bike. (**3**) I .... (eat) an ice cream.

B I'm at the zoo. (**4**) It's warm but it .... (rain). (**5**) I .... (carry) my umbrella. (**6**) I .... (not wear) my sunglasses. (**7**) The lions .... (run) and (**8**) the kangaroos .... (jump).

C I'm in the mountains. (**9**) It's cold but it .... (not snow). (**10**) My brother .... (climb) a mountain and (**11**) my sister .... (ski).

4 Choose and write the correct form.

read   sit   laugh   ~~rain~~   sleep   swim   run   have   ~~shine~~   eat

Dear Sue

I'm at the beach. (**1**) It ...isn't raining... . It's hot and sunny.
(**2**) The sun ....is shining.... . (**3**) My grandpa ....
on a chair. (**4**) He .... a book.
(**5**) He .... (**6**) My mum ....
an ice cream. (**7**) My cousins .... in the
sea. (**8**) Two boys .... a race on the
beach. (**9**) They .... I'm not bored.
(**10**) I .... lots of fun.
Love,   Tom

What about you?

5 Write a postcard. Answer the questions. Use ideas from Exercises 3 and 4. Draw or stick a photo.

1 Where are you?   **2** What's the weather like?   **3** What are people doing?

I'm at ....
It ....
My ....
....
I'm ....
Love, ...

① Find the odd one out. Write.

1	strawberry	apple	banana	(saucepan)	saucepan
2	shopping	school	library	supermarket	....
3	mountain	ski	river	forest	....
4	chase	move	taste	rope	....
5	brave	tired	thief	bored	....

② Read and write. Then look and match.

Fido   Jim   Tom   John   Susan   Anna

1 Susan ....is helping.... (help) her mum with the shopping. She .... (carry) a big shopping bag.

2 Tom .... (not talk) to his friends. He .... (talk) on the phone.

3 Jim .... (not buy) bananas. He .... (buy) strawberries.

4 John .... (ride) a bike but he .... (not be) very good.

5 Fido .... (chase) a cat. He .... (not walk) quietly.

6 Anna and her friends .... (wait) for a bus. She .... (not wear) a dress. She .... (wear) shorts.

③ Look at Exercise 2. Write questions and answers.

1 Susan / carry / a small bag?

   Is Susan carrying a small bag?   No, she isn't. She's

2 Tom / talk / on the phone?

   ....

3 Jim / buy / bananas?

....

4 John / ride / a bike?

....

5 Fido / chase / a thief?

....

6 Anna / wear / a dress?

....

4 **Look, choose and write. Use** Let's **and** Don't.

fight   ~~play volleyball~~   swim   be scared   have an ice cream   chase the dog

Let's play volleyball.

My English

Read and colour.

1 He isn't eating apples. He's eating oranges.

2 Are you watching TV? Yes, I am. / No, I'm not.

3 It's hot. Let's go to the beach.

4 Sit down. Don't sit down.

He's got my toothbrush.

1 **Read and write.**

a towel

a concert

a bed

~~argue~~

a saucepan

a toothbrush

shampoo

supermarket

1 You do this when you're angry.   argue
2 You wash your hair with this.   ....
3 You clean your teeth with this.   ....
4 You cook soup in this.   ....
5 You can sit on this at the beach.   ....
6 You can see a band here.   ....
7 You sleep in this.   ....

2 **Read and draw.**

1 It's half past one.   **2** It's half past three.   **3** It's half past six.   **4** It's half past ten.

3 **Look and write.**

1 It's half past two.   **2** ....   **3** ....

4 ....   **5** ....   **6** ....

4 **Match and write.**

1 ___I___ 'm a tiger.
2 _____'s a frog.
3 _____'s wearing a T-shirt.
4 _____'re listening to music.
5 _____'ve got a new bike.
6 _____'s reading a book and laughing.
7 _____'re walking to school.

a Our school is near our house.
b Their favourite band is the Fly High band.
c My name is Tag.
d Its body is green.
e His T-shirt is yellow.
f Your bike is blue.
g Her book is funny.

5 **Read and write. Use** my, your, her, its, our **or** their.

A: Hello. I'm Kate. What's (**1**) __your__ name?
B: (**2**) _____ name is Ben. Nice to meet you.
A: Have you and your brother got a dog?
B: Yes, we have. (**3**) _____ dog is funny. (**4**) _____ ears are very long.
A: Who's that girl? Is she (**5**) _____ sister?
B: No, she isn't. She's my friend. (**6**) _____ name is Karen.
A: Are they your cousins?
B: Yes, they are. (**7**) _____ dad is my uncle.

6 **Read, choose and write.**

We're at a concert today. We're listening to
(**1**) __our__ favourite band.
I'm wearing (**2**) _____ new T-shirt. It's got
a picture of the band on it.
There are lots of people at the concert.
They're clapping (**3**) _____ hands.
My sister is dancing with (**4**) _____ friends.
My brother is playing (**5**) _____ guitar.
He's in the band! (**6**) _____ name is the Fly
High band.
What about you? What's (**7**) _____
favourite band?

1	(our)	your	their
2	his	her	my
3	our	your	their
4	his	her	my
5	his	her	my
6	His	Her	Its
7	our	your	their

14 This is Trumpet's trumpet.

1 Look and circle.

Chatter

Trumpet

Karla

Patty

Tag

1 Patty has got a trumpet / (tambourine.)
2 Chatter is playing the drums / guitar.
3 Karla is playing the keyboard / trumpet.

4 Tag has got a tambourine / guitar.
5 Trumpet is playing his trumpet / drums.
6 The Fly High Band are brave / ready to play their new song!

2 Look and write.

1 What's this?
   It's ....Tag's guitar....... .

2 What's this?
   It's ....

3 What's this?
   It's ....

4 What's this?
   It's ....

5 What's this?
   It's ....

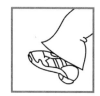

6 What's this?
   It's ....

3 Look and answer the questions.

Nod

Bob

1 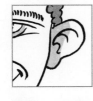 Whose ear is this?
It's Nod's ear.

2  Whose mouth is this?
....

3 Whose nose is this?
....

4 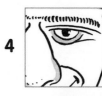 Whose eye is this?
....

5  Whose nose is this?
....

6 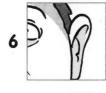 Whose ear is this?
....

7 Whose hair is this?
....

8  Whose hair is this?
....

4 Write questions and answers.

1 dolls Whose dolls are these? They're Rosie's dolls.
2 bike ....
3 robot ....
4 balls ....
5 rollerblades ....
6 kite ....

15 We've got some oranges.

1 Look, circle and write.

1 They've got (some) / any
_____oranges_____ .

2 They haven't got some / any
_____ .

3 They've got some / any
_____ .

4 They've got some / any
_____ .

5 They haven't got some / any
_____ .

6 They haven't got some / any
_____ .

7 They've got some / any
_____ .

8 They haven't got some / any
_____ .

2 Read and write some or any. Then tick (✓) and answer

Trumpet: I'm thirsty. Have we got (**1**) __any__ juice?

Karla: No, we haven't. But we can make juice. Have we got (**2**) _____ oranges?

Trumpet: Yes, we have. We've got (**3**) _____ peaches and (**4**) _____ watermelons too.

Karla: Have we got (**5**) _____ apples?

Trumpet: No, we haven't got (**6**) _____ apples and we haven't got (**7**) _____ bananas.

Karla: That's OK. Have we got (**8**) _____ strawberries?

Trumpet: Yes, we have.

JUNGLE JUICE
oranges ....✓....
peaches ....
watermelons ....
strawberries ....

Can Trumpet and Karla make Jungle Juice? _____

3 Look, choose and write.

photos   eggs   dishes   sweets   books   ~~peaches~~   glasses

1 There are some _____ oranges and
some peaches _____ in the bowl but
there aren't any _____ watermelons.

2 _____ carrots and
_____ in the fridge but
_____ strawberries.

3 _____ and
_____ in the cupboard but
_____ straws.

4 _____ and
_____ on the shelf but
_____ .

4 Look at Exercise 3. Write questions and answers.

1 carrots / fridge?   Are there any carrots in the fridge?   Yes, there are.   .
2 apples / bowl?   _____   _____
3 straws / cupboard?   _____   _____
4 eggs / fridge?   _____   _____
5 peaches / bowl?   _____   _____
6 sweets / shelf?   _____   _____

5 Write about you.

1 peaches / my school bag   There _____ .
2 books / my bedroom   _____
3 toys / my cupboard   _____
4 chairs / our bathroom   _____
5 trees / our living room   _____
6 supermarkets / our town   _____

16 There isn't much spaghetti.

1 Look and write A or B.

A
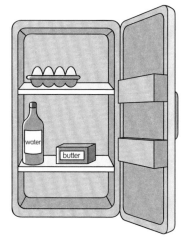

B

1 There's some butter. _____A_____
2 There are some biscuits. _____
3 There's some water. _____

4 There's some flour. _____
5 There are some eggs. _____
6 There's some sugar. _____

2 Look at Exercise 1. Write Is there any or Are there any. Then answer.

In the fridge …
1 ____Is there any____ butter?   ____Yes, there is.____
2 _____ peaches?   ____No, there aren't.____
3 _____ milk?   _____

In the cupboard …
4 _____ honey?   _____
5 _____ biscuits? _____
6 _____ flour?   _____

3 Write the words in the correct box.

~~oranges~~   ~~honey~~
bananas   biscuits
butter   eggs   milk
carrots   flour   sugar
apples   water
cheese   peaches

Countable nouns	Uncountable nouns
There are some …	There's some …
oranges	honey

4 **Look and answer. Use** much, many **or** lots of.

1	How much cheese is there?	There's ....lots of........ cheese.
2	How many eggs are there?	There aren't .... eggs.
3	How much milk is there?	There isn't .... milk.
4	How many biscuits are there?	There are .... biscuits.

5 **Look at Exercise 4. Write and answer.**

1 ....How much.... bread ....is there.... ? ....There's lots of bread....

2 .... apples .... ?

3 .... spaghetti .... ?

4 .... strawberries .... ?

6 **Write** How much **or** How many **and answer the questions.**

1 ....How many.... legs has an octopus got?
....It's got....

2 .... brothers have you got?

3 .... water do you drink every day?

4 .... children are there in your class?

5 .... juice is there in your fridge at home?

6 .... money does a cinema ticket cost?

The babies are hungry!

1 Look and write.

1 ....sheep.... ....sheep....   **2** ....

3 ....   **4** ....

5 ....   **6** ....

2 Read and answer.

1 Are the babies mice?
....No, they aren't....
What are the babies drinking?
....They're drinking milk....

2 Are the babies foxes?
....
What are they eating?
....

3 Are the babies sheep?
....
What are they eating?
....

4 Are the babies wolves?
....
What are they eating?
....

3 Choose and write.

isn't   many   lots of   eggs   there   much   lots

Peter is having breakfast. What's on the table this morning? There are two (**1**) _____eggs_____ on the table. There's (**2**) _____ bread. How (**3**) _____ butter is there? There's (**4**) _____ of butter. How (**5**) _____ oranges are there? There are three oranges. How much milk is (**6**) _____? There (**7**) _____ much milk.

4 Look, read and write.

I eat three meals every day. For breakfast I have some (**1**) _____bread_____ with lots of (**2**) _____ and (**3**) _____. I don't drink any (**4**) _____, but I drink some juice.
For lunch I have some (**5**) _____ and I have an (**6**) _____ too.
For dinner I have some (**7**) _____ with (**8**) _____ or some (**9**) _____ with (**10**) _____.
I don't eat much (**11**) _____ and I don't eat many (**12**) _____, but I eat lots of (**13**) _____. I drink lots of (**14**) _____.

What about you?

5 Write about what you eat every day. Draw or stick pictures.

I eat three meals every day. For breakfast _____
_____ .
For lunch _____
_____ .
For dinner _____
_____ .
I don't eat _____
_____ .

The **FlyHigh** Review 4

1 Write.

Instruments → I   making a Cake → C   parts of the Body → B   BathTime → BT

head _____ B	shampoo _____	mouth _____	eggs _____
drums _____	keyboard _____	sugar _____	toothbrush _____
flour _____	tambourine _____	butter _____	ears _____
trumpet _____	towel _____	nose _____	water _____

2 Write. Then match.

1 It's _half past seven._

2 It's _____ .

3 It's _____ .

4 It's _____ .

a I'm going to bed.

b I'm having lunch.

c I'm having breakfast.

d I'm doing my homework.

3 Read, choose and write.

Whose   's   His   her   my   Their   ~~your~~   's

A: Look! There's Fiona.

B: I don't know Fiona. (**1**) Is she __your__ friend?

A: Yes, she is. (**2**) She's _____ best friend. Look. (**3**) She's playing _____ guitar now.

A: Oh yes. Who's the boy with Fiona?

B: (**4**) That's Fiona _____ brother. (**5**) _____ name is Mark.

A: (**6**) _____ keyboard is that?

B: (**7**) It's Mark _____ keyboard.

A: Are Fiona and Mark in a band?

B: Yes, they are. (**8**) _____ music is great.

4 **Look and write. Use** There's lots of, There isn't much, There are lots of **or** There aren't many.

1   There's lots of spaghetti.
2   ....
3   ....
4   ....
5   ....
6   ....

5 **Write the plurals in the correct box.**

~~baby~~ ~~wolf~~ ~~person~~ ~~tomato~~ mouse sheep leaf potato
sandwich foot cherry peach thief strawberry tooth

~~y~~ + –ies	+ –es	~~f~~ + –ves	irregular
babies	tomatoes	wolves	people

6 **Read and write. Use words from Exercise 5.**

1 These animals are grey. They chase sheep. They're .... wolves ....
2 These animals are very small. They like cheese. They're ....
3 We sometimes eat these for lunch. They're ....
4 The police don't always catch these people. They're ....
5 These are in your mouth. They're ....

My English

Read and colour.

1 Katie has got a dog. This is Katie's dog.   :| :)   :D

2 We've got some bananas but we haven't got any peaches.   :| :)   :D

3 Is there any cheese in the fridge? Yes, there is. / No, there isn't.   :| :)   :D

17 Trumpet is stronger.

1 **Do the crossword.**

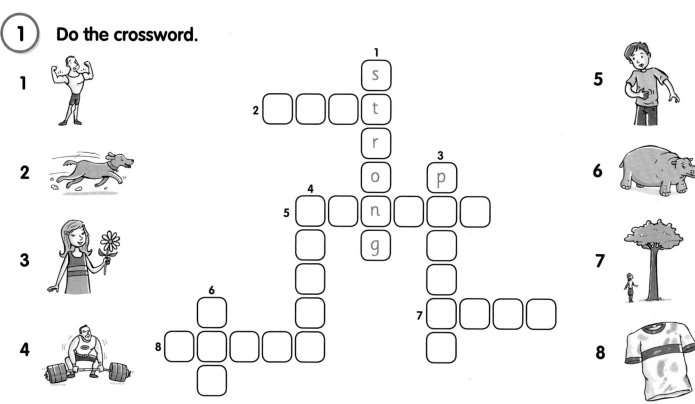

2 **Read and draw.**

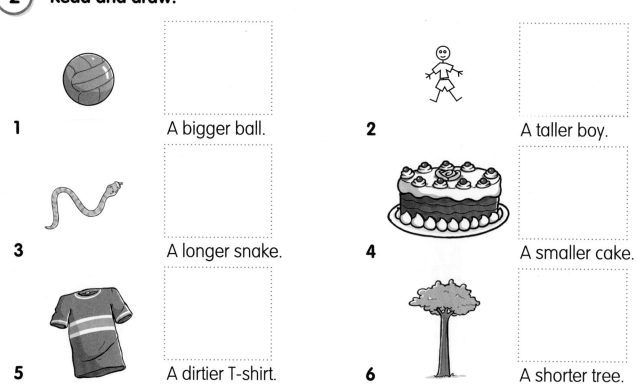

1 A bigger ball.

2 A taller boy.

3 A longer snake.

4 A smaller cake.

5 A dirtier T-shirt.

6 A shorter tree.

3 Write.

1 Footballs are _____bigger_____ (big) than tennis balls.
2 Trains are _____ (slow) than planes.
3 Tigers are _____ (fast) than penguins.
4 Turkey is _____ (hot) than Britain.
5 The green team is _____ (good) than the yellow team.
6 The blue team is _____ (bad) than the white team.

4 Write and answer.

1 Is the clown _____taller_____ (tall) than the cowboy? _____Yes, he is._____
2 Is the dancer _____ (pretty) than the pirate? _____
3 Is the cowboy _____ (small) than the pirate? _____
4 Is the queen _____ (short) than the king? _____
5 Is the dog _____ (heavy) than the cat? _____
6 Is the cat _____ (dirty) than the dog? _____

5 Write about you.

1 My mum / tall / me _____My mum is taller than me._____
2 I / short / my dad _____
3 My grandma / old / my mum _____
4 My dad's car / fast / my bike _____
5 The park / big / my garden _____
6 My house / small / my school _____

(18) The best zoo in the world.

1 Find and write the opposites.

h	n	u	y	c	t	m	p	o
a	t	u	i	n	o	i	s	y
p	h	j	s	o	m	t	b	o
p	i	v	e	b	o	s	b	u
y	n	p	u	q	g	m	r	n
h	i	c	o	l	d	a	j	g
l	j	g	d	a	z	l	c	z
s	h	o	r	t	f	l	r	p

1 sad .... happy ....
2 fat ....
3 old ....
4 hot ....
5 long ....
6 big ....
7 quiet ....

2 Write.

old	1 ...... older	the oldest
2	3	the fastest
clever	4	5 ....

big	6	the biggest
thin	thinner	7 ....
8	hotter	9 ....

happy	10	the happiest
11	prettier	12 ....
13	heavier	14 ....

good	15	the best
bad	worse	16 ....

3 Write. Use words from Exercise 2.

1 Tom is ...... the oldest ...... (old) pupil in our class.
2 Paul is .... (good) player in our team.
3 Chatter is .... (bad) singer in the zoo.
4 My mum is .... (clever) person in my family.
5 August is .... (hot) month of the year in England.

4 Do the quiz. Choose and write.

small ~~strong~~ clever big funny tall

1 Elephants are the ......strongest...... animals in the world.
2 Whales are the .... animals in the sea.
3 Giraffes are the .... animals in the zoo.
4 Penguins are the .... birds in the zoo.
5 Insects are the .... animals in the zoo.
6 Dolphins are the .... animals in the sea.

5 Look and write.

1		
Katie	Rosa	Sally
slow		fast
Katie ....is slower than.... Rosa.
Rosa ....is faster than.... Katie.
Sally ....is the fastest.... . She's the winner.

2		
Britain 20°C	Turkey 30°C	Africa 40°C
cold		hot
Britain .... Turkey.
Turkey .... Britain.
Africa .... It's very sunny.

3		
rhino	elephant	giraffe
short		tall
The rhino .... the elephant.
The elephant .... the rhino.
The giraffe .... It's got a long neck.

4		
Rover	Fido	Max
thin		fat
Rover .... Fido.
Fido .... Rover.
Max .... He eats a lot.

6 Answer about you.

1 Who's the oldest person in your family? ....The oldest person in my family is.... .
2 Who's the tallest person in your family? ....The tallest person is.................... .
3 Who's the funniest person in your family? ....
4 Who's the worst singer in your family? ....
5 What's the hottest month of the year? ....
6 What's the coldest month of the year? ....

19 We were in the playground.

1 Put the letters in the correct order. Choose and write.

ddlemi   ycr   glpaudyron   ngierf   aecicdnt   ~~uersn~~

1 My mum isn't a teacher. She's a ......nurse...... .
2 There are three houses. My house is in the ....
3 I can't play the guitar now. Look at my ....
4 Look, an ....! Let's call for help.
5 You're sad. Please don't ....
6 We always play in the .... at lunch time.

2 Look, read and circle.

Yesterday …

1 The children was / (were) at the playground.   2 The girl was / were on the slide.

3 The boy was / were on his bike.   4 They was / were on the swings.

3 Write was or were. Then number.

   1

1 On Sunday Charles ...was... in the forest. The leaves .... red and yellow.
2 In winter Charles .... in the mountains. It .... very cold.
3 On Friday Charles and his dad .... in town. They .... at the shops.
4 In summer Charles .... at the beach. It .... very sunny.

4 **Read and write** was **or** were.

It (**1**) ...was... half past two in the afternoon on Sunday. Lots of visitors (**2**) .... at the zoo. Rob and Vicky and their friends (**3**) .... in the playground. Tag (**4**) .... on his bike. Chatter (**5**) .... on his rollerblades. There (**6**) .... an accident and Vicky (**7**) .... in the middle. The nurse (**8**) .... very good and Vicky is at home now.

5 **Read Exercise 4 again. Write** yes **or** no.

1 Lots of visitors were at the zoo on Monday afternoon. ...no...
2 Rob was in the playground with Vicky and their friends. ....
3 Tag and Chatter were on their rollerblades. ....
4 Vicky was in an accident. ....
5 Vicky is at school now. ....

6 **Choose and write.**

am   is   are
1 Today I ...am... at the park.
2 Today we .... in the library.
3 It .... hot and sunny today.
4 Rob and Vicky .... at the zoo today.
5 Vicky .... a pretty girl.
6 I .... happy today.

was   were
Yesterday I ...was... at school.
On Saturday we .... at the cinema.
It .... rainy yesterday.
They .... at the zoo yesterday, too.
She .... a pretty baby, too.
Yesterday I .... tired.

7 **Write. Then tick (✓) or cross (✗) for you.**

1 I / at school / on Monday   I was at school on Monday. ....
2 My dad / at the zoo / on Sunday ....
3 My friends / in the park / this morning ....
4 I / happy / on Friday ....
5 My mum / tired / on Wednesday ....
6 It / sunny / on Saturday ....

(20) There weren't any chocolates.

(1) Match and write.

 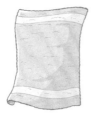  

1 They're fruit. They're green or purple. ....grapes........
2 This is long and thin. A nurse puts it on you. ....
3 This is part of your body. It's got fingers. ....
4 It comes when there's an accident. ....
5 It's the day before today. ....
6 These are part of your hand. ....

(2) Correct the sentences.

1 He was at school yesterday.
   He wasn't at school yesterday.
   He was at home.

2 They were in the kitchen yesterday evening.
   ....
   ....

3 We were at the zoo on Saturday.
   ....
   ....

4 He was at the cinema yesterday.
   ....
   ....

3 **Look, read and circle.**

1 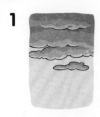  2   3   4

1 Was it cloudy yesterday? (Yes, it was.) / No, it wasn't.
2 Was Anna in the playground? Yes, she was. / No, she wasn't.
3 Was she with her friends? Yes, she was. / No, she wasn't.
4 Were they happy? Yes, they were. / No, they weren't.

4 **Write the questions in the correct order. Then answer about you.**

1 school / at / yesterday? / you / Were
   Were you at school yesterday? ....

2 in the park / Were / friends / yesterday? / your
   ....

3 cold / yesterday? / Was / it
   ....

4 yesterday? / you / sad / Were
   ....

5 your / Was / at / yesterday? / mum / home
   ....

6 the / your / Was / dad / yesterday? / garden / in
   ....

5 **Look and write. Use** There was**,** There were **or** There weren't**.**

It was sunny yesterday afternoon.
1 ___There weren't___ any clouds in the sky.
2 .... some children in the playground.
3 .... a girl on the slide.
4 .... two boys on the climbing frame.
5 .... any dogs in the playground.
6 .... a cat under the climbing frame.
7 .... two bikes next to the slide.

Amazing world

1 Write and match.

a

b

c
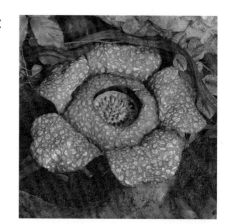

d

e

f

1 This is the ....*oldest*.......... (old) lake in the world. ....*f*.......
2 This is the .... (small) bird in the world. ....
3 He was the .... (tall) man in the world. ....
4 This is the .... (fast) animal in the world. ....
5 This is the .... (big) flower in the world. ....
6 She was the .... (young) person to win a gold medal in the Olympics. ....

2 Write.

34	*thirty-four*	55	
	sixty-five	82	
79			seventy-three
48		99	
	twenty-one	100	

3 Look, read and write.

Jonathan is my grandpa. He's the tallest person in the family. He's one metre and eighty-two centimetres tall. My grandma, Tania, is one metre and sixty-three centimetres tall. My father, Sam, is one metre and seventy-nine centimetres tall. His sister, Katie, is one metre and fifty-nine centimetres tall.

Jonathan	1 metre	82	centimetres
Tania	1 metre	....	centimetres
Sam	1 metre	....	centimetres
Katie	1 metre	....	centimetres

4 Look, read and write.

Saturday
morning
library
afternoon
shops
evening
7.30 cinema with friends

Sunday
morning
10.00 park
afternoon
zoo
evening
6.30 home with family

On Saturday I was very busy. In the morning I was at (1) ..... the library .
In the afternoon I was at (2) ....
At (3) .... in the evening, I was at (4) .... with my friends.
On Sunday I was busy too. At (5) .... in the morning I was in (6) .... I was at (7) .... in the afternoon. At (8) .... in the evening I was at (9) .... with my family.

What about you?

5 Complete the diary. Then write about your last weekend. Use Exercise 4 as a model.

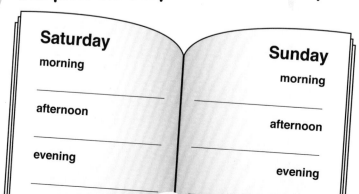

Saturday
morning
_____
afternoon
_____
evening
_____

Sunday
morning
_____
afternoon
_____
evening
_____

On Saturday I was very busy.
....
....
On Sunday ....
....
....

1 Find the odd one out. Write.

1 ambulance	(heavy)	nurse	accident	heavy
2 rhino	giraffe	finger	hummingbird	
3 chocolates	seventy-six	strawberries	cherries	
4 thirty-eight	fifty-four	ninety-two	bandage	
5 grapes	hand	head	leg	

2 Read and write.

Blue whales are (**1**) ...the biggest... (big) animals in the world. Killer whales are big dolphins. They are (**2**) .... (small) than blue whales but they are (**3**) .... (fast) animals in the sea. They can swim at (**4**) .... (55) kilometres per hour. Whales are (**5**) .... (loud) and (**6**) .... (noisy) animals in the world. They sing songs and talk to each other! They make the (**7**) .... (long) journeys too. Some whales swim from the Pacific Ocean to the Atlantic Ocean every year!

3 Look at the table. Write sentences.

	How old?	How tall?	How heavy?
Kevin	10	1 metre 55 centimetres	45 kilos
Peter	9	1 metre 50 centimetres	40 kilos
Rosa	8	1 metre 45 centimetres	38 kilos
Mary	12	1 metre 64 centimetres	51 kilos

1 Kevin / Peter (old) Kevin is older than Peter.
2 Rosa / Mary (tall) ....
3 Peter / Rosa (heavy) ....
4 Rosa / Peter (short) ....
5 Mary / Rosa (young) ....
6 (heavy) Mary is the heaviest.   **8** (tall) ....
7 (young) ....   **9** (short) ....

4 **Read and write** was, wasn't or were. **Then number.**

1 **2**  **3**  **4**

Saturday

On Saturday morning I (**1**) ....was............ in the playground with my friends. It was a sunny day and we (**2**) .... on the swings. It (**3**) .... fun. | 4 |

In the afternoon I (**4**) .... at the supermarket with my mum. I don't like shopping. I (**5**) .... bored. It (**6**) .... fun. ☐

Sunday

On Sunday morning I (**7**) .... at home with my family. ☐

In the afternoon I (**8**) .... at the aquarium with my friends. The sharks (**9**) .... very big. We (**10**) .... scared! But we (**11**) .... very brave! ☐

Jill

5 **Read Exercise 4 again. Write** Was **or** Were **and answer.**

1 ......Was...... it sunny on Saturday? ......Yes, it was.......

2 .... Jill and her friends at the zoo in the morning?
......No,...................... . They............................... .

3 .... she excited at the supermarket? ....

4 .... she at the library on Sunday morning? ....

5 .... she at the aquarium on Sunday afternoon? ....

6 .... the sharks big? ....

7 .... Jill and her friends brave? ....

My English

Read and colour.

1 Trains are faster than planes.

2 Sue is the tallest girl in my school.

3 I was at the beach yesterday. I wasn't at the library. ☺ ☺ ☺

4 Were there many people at the beach?
Yes, there were. / No, there weren't. ☺ ☺ ☺

FUN TIME 2

1 **Find and circle. Then say.**

1   ph

2   ch

3   sh

4   th

3+5=8

2 **Put the letters in the correct order. Write the words in the correct box.**

~~hnepo~~   thaMs   alctohoce   ishd   tifhe   telahbap   omapsoh   ncuhl

ph	ch	sh	th
phone			

3 **Find and write the opposites**

         hot   cold

tall   slow   thin   old   fat   small

young   big   ~~hot~~   short   ~~cold~~   fast

4 **Write.**

1 Four things smaller than you: ....

2 Four things faster than you: ....

3 Four things heavier than you: ....

4 Four people older than you: ....

5 **Do the quiz. Choose and write.**

1 Lake Baikal is .... lake in the world.
  a the newest   **b** the biggest   **c** the oldest

2 The Blue Whale is .... animal in the world.
  a the smallest   **b** the biggest   **c** the fastest

3 The Amazon is .... river in the world.
  a the shortest   **b** the longest   **c** the thinnest

4 The cheetah is .... animal in the world.
  a the fastest   **b** the slowest   **c** the fattest

5 Mount Everest is .... mountain in the world.
  a the shortest   **b** the smallest   **c** the tallest

6 The elephant is .... animal in the world.
  a the smallest   **b** the strongest   **c** the slowest

6 **Do the crossword and answer the question.**

1 We're .... TV in the living room now.

2 You're taller .... me.

3 ' .... pen is this?' 'It's my pen.'

4 How .... milk is there?

5 There are .... peaches in the bowl.

6 I've got .... of friends.

7 There .... a big dog in the park yesterday.

8 They've got a radio. It's .... radio.

9 The children .... happy yesterday.

Do you like .... ? ....

21 We danced in the Olympics.

1 Circle. Then choose and write.

a

zookeeper /
~~photographer~~ (circled)

b

newspaper / book

c

teacher / reporter

d

postman /
police officer

1 A ...... photographer ...... takes photos for a newspaper.
2 A .... writes stories for a newspaper.
3 A .... works in a school. He or she helps children learn new things.
4 A .... works in a zoo. He or she looks after animals.
5 A .... carries letters, postcards and parcels to your home.
6 A .... chases thieves.

2 Choose and write. Then look and number.

helped   visited   played   listened
~~cleaned~~   watched

Yesterday Megan was very busy.
1 In the morning she ...... cleaned ...... her bedroom.
2 Then she .... her mum.
3 Then she .... volleyball with her friend.
4 In the afternoon she .... her aunt and uncle.
5 In the evening she .... TV.
6 Then she .... to music.

3 Match.

Yesterday …
1 we walked
2 we cooked
3 we climbed
4 we washed
5 we talked
6 we danced

a some spaghetti.
b to our friends.
c the kitchen floor.
d to school.
e in the living room.
f a tree.

4 **What did Jack do last Saturday? Read and write. Use the past tense.**

Saturday

9.00 clean bedroom
10.00 play the guitar
12.30 help Dad in the garden
2.00 visit grandma
5.00 cook spaghetti with Mum
6.30 play computer games

Jack was very busy last Saturday.

1 _At 9 o'clock he cleaned his bedroom._
2 ....
3 ....
4 ....
5 ....
6 ....

5 **Read, choose and write the past tense forms.**

play   help   listen   wash   play   ~~wash~~   walk   dance   talk

On Saturday morning I **(1)** _washed_ my hair. Then I **(2)** .... my mum in the kitchen. After lunch I **(3)** .... the dishes.
In the afternoon my friend and I **(4)** .... to the park. We **(5)** .... on the swings and then we **(6)** .... a game of football. In the evening I **(7)** .... to my grandma on the phone. Then I **(8)** .... to music and I **(9)** .... in my bedroom. It was a very nice day.

6 **Write the sentences. Then tick (✓) or cross (✗) about you.**

1 I / paint / a picture / yesterday   _I painted a picture yesterday._ ....
2 My friends / visit / me / on Sunday ....
3 My dad / work / on Saturday ....
4 My mum / cook / pizza / yesterday ....
5 I / climb / a tree / on Monday ....
6 I / talk / to my friends / yesterday ....

1 **Choose and write.**

wet   accident   ~~mess~~   wash   clean up   mind

1   Look at the floor! What a ....mess........ .

2   Never .... It was an ....

3   Let's help Sally to ....

4   OK. You can .... the floor.

5   Be careful! Don't walk on the floor, now. It's ....

2 **Look, choose and write about yesterday.**

didn't play / played   didn't wash / washed   didn't clean / cleaned
~~didn't climb / climbed~~   didn't walk / walked   didn't wait / waited

1   He ....didn't climb.... a mountain.
He ....climbed.... a tree.

2   She .... the floor.
She .... her teeth.

3   They .... volleyball.
They .... tennis.

4   He .... for a train.
He .... for a bus.

5   They .... on the beach.
They .... in the park.

6   She .... the dishes.
She .... her hair.

3 **Look and write.**

My family yesterday

1 Mum / cook dinner / play the drums

Mum didn't cook dinner yesterday. She played the drums.

2 Grandma / take photos / paint a picture

....

3 Dad / clean the windows / wash the floor

....

4 Grandpa / work in the garden / jump in the living room

....

4 **Look at Exercise 3. Write and answer.**

1 ...Did... Grandma watch TV yesterday? ...No, she didn't.

2 .... Grandma paint a picture? ...Yes, she did.

3 .... Dad wash his hair? ....

4 .... Dad clean the windows? ....

5 .... Grandpa cook the dinner? ....

6 .... Grandpa jump? ....

7 .... Mum play the guitar? ....

8 .... Mum play the drums? ....

5 **Write the questions in the correct order. Then answer about you.**

1 you / Did / wash / yesterday? / your hair

Did you wash your hair yesterday? ....

2 the windows / Did / on Sunday? / your dad / clean

....

3 play / on Saturday? / in the park / your friends / Did

....

4 on Friday? / visit / Did / your grandma

....

We had a wonderful time.

1 **Find and write the past tense forms.**

```
t  b  o  p  f  g  e  r  e  a  d
o  p  t (c  a  m  e) w  w  s  p
o  v  z  r  m  a  q  h  r  q  s
k  w  e  n  t  x  m  b  o  d  b
m  o  s  a  w  s  h  j  t  l  o
z  y  p  b  u  r  a  n  e  d  u
o  x  t  j  m  r  d  u  i  o  g
d  w  m  a  d  e  t  g  r  f  h
i  s  r  t  z  o  b  j  s  a  t
d  u  j  e  f  m  n  p  z  r  f
n  g  o  t  v  d  r  a  n  k  o
```

1 come ......came...... **9** make ....

2 buy .... **10** read ....

3 do .... **11** see ....

4 drink .... **12** sit ....

5 eat .... **13** take ....

6 get up .... up **14** write ....

7 go .... **15** run ....

8 have ....

2 **Write the correct present or past forms.**

1 have

I ....had.... a party last Saturday. I always ....have.... a party for my birthday.

2 drink

We .... milk for breakfast yesterday. We .... milk every morning.

3 read

Mum .... the newspaper this morning. She .... the newspaper every day.

4 do

I .... my homework at half past five. I .... my homework every evening.

5 eat

We .... pizza on Friday evening. We always .... pizza on Friday.

6 go

Dad .... to the supermarket yesterday. He .... to the supermarket every week.

3 Look, choose and write the past tense forms. Then number.

eat   see   buy   have   ~~drink~~   take

There were lots of children at the beach last Saturday.

1 Sue and Tom ....._drank_..... some water. **4** Paul, Katie and John .... a picnic.

2 Sam and Peter .... a dolphin. **5** John .... a sandwich.

3 Kevin .... some photos. **6** Harry and Emily .... some oranges.

4 Read, choose and write the past tense forms.

have   have   come   buy   ~~go~~   see   make   take   take   write

I (**1**) ....._went_..... to the zoo last Sunday with my family. My friends
(**2**) .... with us. My mum (**3**) .... some sandwiches
and we (**4**) .... our cameras. We (**5**) .... giraffes and
elephants and lots of other animals. We (**6**) .... lots of photos.
We (**7**) .... a picnic at two o'clock. Then I (**8**) ....
some postcards and I (**9**) .... a postcard to my penfriend in
Russia. We (**10**) .... a great day.

5 Choose and write about you.

1 I ....._ate_..................... yesterday. a sandwich / an apple / some chocolate

2 I .... this morning. some milk / some water / some juice

3 I .... on Friday. to school / to the park / to the cinema

4 I .... last weekend. a shower / a picnic / a party

5 I .... yesterday. a book / a newspaper / a letter

6 I .... on Sunday. my friends / my cousins / my grandma

24 Did you drink your milk?

1 **Do the crossword. Write.**

The secret word is ....

2 **Read. Then correct the sentences.**

Last Sunday, my dad and I went for a walk in the forest. My mum made some sandwiches for us. I took my camera and my dad took a map. We saw a bear. I was scared but the bear ran away. We ate our sandwiches for lunch.

1 Last Sunday Tom and his dad went to the beach.
They ____didn't go____ to the beach. They ____went____ for a walk in the forest.

2 His mum made pizza for them.
She .... pizza for them. She ....

3 Tom took his phone.
He .... his phone. He ....

4 His dad took his passport.
He .... his passport. He ....

5 They saw a giraffe.
They .... a giraffe. They ....

6 Tom was happy.
Tom .... happy. He ....

7 The bear chased them.
The bear .... them. It .... away.

3 Read and write the past tense forms.

My name is Paul. Last summer I (**1**) ....went.......... (go) to the beach with my family. It (**2**) .... (be) sunny and hot. My mum and dad (**3**) .... (sit) on the sand.
Mum (**4**) .... (read) a book.
Dad (**5**) .... (drink) some juice.
My sister and I (**6**) .... (swim) in the sea. We (**7**) .... (not see) any fish in the sea but we (**8**) .... (see) a big crab on the beach. I (**9**) .... (eat) a chocolate ice cream. We (**10**) .... (have) a great day.

4 Look at Exercise 3 and answer.

1 Did Paul and his family go to the beach last summer? ....Yes, they did...........
2 Did his mum and dad swim in the sea? ....No, they didn't. They..........
3 Did his dad read a book? ....
4 Did Paul and his sister swim in the sea? ....
5 Did they see any fish in the sea? ....
6 Did Paul eat a strawberry ice cream? ....

5 Write the questions in the correct order. Then answer about you.

1 get up / Did / this morning? / you / early
..........Did you get up early this morning?..........

2 you / for breakfast? / have / Did / pizza
....

3 ride / Did / your bike / to school? / you
....

4 last night? / you / your homework / do / Did
....

5 your best friend / see / Did / you / this morning?
....

6 an apple / yesterday? / you / eat / Did
....

Sally's Story
A week in London

1 **Look and match.**

1st 2nd 3rd 4th 5th 6th

fourth second last fifth first sixth third

2 **Write. Then match.**

1

2

3

4

5

6

7

1	On the ___first___ day Sam and Katie	**a**	went to Madame Tussaud's museum.
2	On the _____ day they	**b**	visited the Natural History Museum.
3	On the _____ day they	**c**	went on the London Eye.
4	On the _____ day they	**d**	went to Hyde Park.
5	On the _____ day they	**e**	went to Oxford Street.
6	On the _____ day they	**f**	visited Buckingham Palace.
7	On the _____ day they	**g**	saw Big Ben.

3 Read and answer.

1 Did Sam and Katie see the Queen at Buckingham Palace? ......No, they didn't.......
2 Did they swim in the Serpentine Lake in Hyde Park? ....
3 Was it 12 o'clock when they saw Big Ben? ....
4 Did they buy postcards at the Natural History Museum? ....
5 Did they see the River Thames? ....
6 Did they like Prince William at Madame Tussaud's Museum? ....
7 Did they go to the cinema on the last day? ....

4 Look, read and write.

Last week our cousins (1) ......came...... (come) to
England for five days. On the first day we went to the
zoo. We (2) .... (see) lots of animals.
On the second day we (3) .... (go) shopping
and my cousins (4) .... (buy) souvenirs.
On the third day my cousins (5) ....
(write) some postcards. On the fourth day we
(6) .... (have) a party. On the last day we
(7) .... (take) our cousins to the airport.

What about you?

5 Write about a visit from your friends or family. Use ideas from Exercise 4. Here are some more ideas. Stick a photo.

go to the museum   go to the circus   swim in the lake   go to the aquarium
ride a horse   see a train   go to a concert   climb a mountain

Last year ....
....
On the first day ....
....
On ....
....
On ....
....

① Look and write.

There was a football game at my school last week.
My (**1**) .... team .... was the best and we were the
(**2**) .... There was a big (**3**) ....
It was a gold cup. We were very happy. The
(**4**) .... of our town was at the game. He likes
football. A (**5**) .... was there too. She asked
us lots of questions. She had a (**6**) .... with
her and our photo was in the (**7**) .... My
mum and dad were very (**8**) .... of me.

② Choose and write.

fourth   ~~first~~   last   sixth   second   third   fifth   ~~1st~~   3rd   5th   6th   2nd   4th

| first 1st | | | | | | |

③ Read, choose and write the correct past tense forms.

watch   make   make   have   have   do   ~~eat~~   ~~eat~~   ride   play   play   walk

Yesterday …

1 I .... ate .... an egg for breakfast. I .... didn't eat .... bread or honey.
2 I .... to school. I .... my bike.
3 In the morning we .... English and Maths. We .... PE.
4 My mum .... cheese sandwiches for my lunch. She ....
chicken sandwiches.
5 After school my friends and I .... tennis in the playground. We
.... volleyball.
6 In the evening I .... my homework. I .... TV.

4 **Look, choose and write the past tense forms.**

swim   write   listen   play   read   s̶i̶t̶   dance   drink   eat   talk

Sam:

Last Saturday my mum took me and my friends to the park. Mum (**1**) ......sat...... under a tree. Kate (**2**) .... on the grass. John and Sue (**3**) .... with a ball. Mark (**4**) .... a book and Emma (**5**) .... to music. Peter (**6**) .... in the pool and Amy (**7**) .... in her book. I (**8**) .... an apple and my best friend (**9**) .... juice. Dan and Tina (**10**) .... and laughed. We had lots of fun!

5 **Read Exercise 4 again. Write questions and answer.**

1 Sam / go to the circus / last Saturday?
Did Sam go to the circus last Saturday?   No, he didn't. He ....

2 Sam's mum / swim / in the pool?
....

3 Mark / read / a newspaper?
....

4 Sam / eat / an orange?
....

5 Amy / write / a postcard?
....

My English

Read and colour.

1 I played with my dog last night. ☺ ☺ ☺

2 Did you listen to music yesterday? Yes, I did. / No, I didn't. ☺ ☺ ☺

3 The children didn't go to school yesterday. They went to the zoo. ☺ ☺ ☺

4 Did you see a whale? Yes, I did. / No, I didn't. ☺ ☺ ☺

25 Can we make a sandcastle?

1 Match and write.

1 You can make this on the beach. _a sandcastle_
2 It's cold and you can eat it. It's yummy! ....
3 You can sit under this on the beach. ....
4 You can put sand in this and make a sandcastle. ....
5 You can wear these in the sea. They help you to swim. ....
6 You can use this to put sand in your bucket. ....
7 It's in the sky. It's hot and yellow. ....

2 Look, read and match.

1 Can I clean the board, please?   _b_
2 Can I go to the bathroom, please?   ....
3 Can I draw a picture, please?   ....
4 Can I open the window, please?   ....

3 Match and write. Use Can I ... , please?

1	have	a	my friend	1	_f_	Can I have an ice cream, please?
2	make	b	a photo	2		
3	phone	c	to the park	3		
4	take	d	in the sea	4		
5	swim	e	a sandcastle	5		
6	go	f	an ice cream	6		

4 **Write and match. Use** can **or** can't.

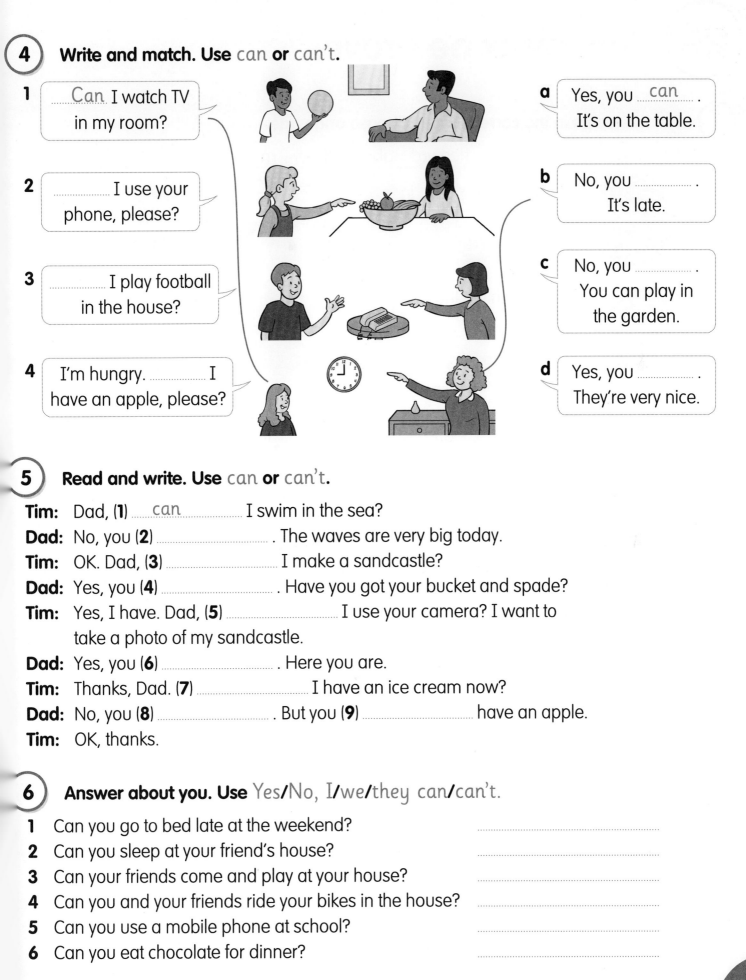

1 Can I watch TV in my room?

2 .... I use your phone, please?

3 .... I play football in the house?

4 I'm hungry. .... I have an apple, please?

a Yes, you can . It's on the table.

b No, you .... It's late.

c No, you .... You can play in the garden.

d Yes, you .... They're very nice.

5 **Read and write. Use** can **or** can't.

Tim: Dad, **(1)** can I swim in the sea?
Dad: No, you **(2)** .... The waves are very big today.
Tim: OK. Dad, **(3)** .... I make a sandcastle?
Dad: Yes, you **(4)** .... Have you got your bucket and spade?
Tim: Yes, I have. Dad, **(5)** .... I use your camera? I want to take a photo of my sandcastle.
Dad: Yes, you **(6)** .... Here you are.
Tim: Thanks, Dad. **(7)** .... I have an ice cream now?
Dad: No, you **(8)** .... But you **(9)** .... have an apple.
Tim: OK, thanks.

6 **Answer about you. Use** Yes/No, I/we/they can/can't.

1 Can you go to bed late at the weekend? ....
2 Can you sleep at your friend's house? ....
3 Can your friends come and play at your house? ....
4 Can you and your friends ride your bikes in the house? ....
5 Can you use a mobile phone at school? ....
6 Can you eat chocolate for dinner? ....

(26) You must be brave.

1 Put the letters in the correct order. Choose and write.

fra   nrae   tonmers   tne   rieowrd   abrev   ttruel   mvoe   ~~csutk~~

1 Help! I'm .....stuck.... in the ....

2 I'm fighting the .... I'm very ....

3 Stop! Don't ....

4 We're .... The shark is .... the beach!

5 We're .... away from home.

6 Is it a crab?

No, it's a ....

2 Read and match.

1
....

2
....

3
.....a.....   ....

a You mustn't feed the animals.
b You mustn't wear flippers.
c You must be quiet.

d You mustn't write in the books.
e You must have a shower before you swim.
f You must buy a ticket.

3 Write must **or** mustn't.

1 You ......must...... clean your teeth every day.
2 You .... play football in the house.
3 You .... help your mum and dad.
4 You .... feed your pets.
5 You .... wear dirty shoes in the house.
6 You .... play computer games all day.

4 Look, choose and write. Use must or mustn't.

~~wear sun cream~~   stay near your family   drink lots of water
sit in the sun   fight   swim far from the beach

At the beach …

1   You must wear sun cream.

2   ....

3   ....

4   ....

5   ....

6   ....

5 Write the school rules. Use must or mustn't.

SCHOOL RULES

1 Don't be late. ✗
2 Sit quietly at your desk. ✓
3 Don't eat food in class. ✗
4 Help each other. ✓
5 Don't draw on the desks. ✗
6 Listen to your teacher. ✓

At school …

1   We mustn't be late.

2   ....

3   ....

4   ....

5   ....

6   ....

6 Tick (✓) or cross (✗). Then write about the library.

1   shout .... ✗ .... You mustn't shout.

2   be quiet ....

3   phone your friends ....

4   eat food ....

5   be careful with the books ....

6   run ....

27 You're safe with us, Carrie.

1 Circle. Then choose and write.

a
(safe) / save

b
fireman / fisherman

c
boat / train

d
argue / ask

e
save / stay

f
near / far

1 Don't be scared. You're ....safe.......... with me.
2 He gets fish from the sea. He's a ....
3 We can go to sea in a ....
4 Let's .... Mum to help us.
5 We're trying to .... a turtle.
6 I can't walk to school. It's too ....

2 Match.

1 I'm strong.
2 You're behind the tree.
3 He's my friend.
4 She's my sister.
5 We can't swim.
6 They're funny.

a Please help us.
b Listen to them.
c I can see you.
d I like him.
e Do you know her?
f Look at me.

3 Choose and write.

me   it   him   her   us   ~~them~~

1 They're on the beach. The dog is chasing .. them.. .
2 He's swimming. Can you see ....?
3 I'm doing a handstand. Look at ....
4 We're playing volleyball. Please take a photo of ....
5 She's sleeping. The baby is next to ....
6 Where's the boat? I can't see ....

4 Read and write.

1 Chatter's got a lot of **bananas**. He's eating ..._them_.. .
2 Sally is phoning **Rob**. She wants to talk to ....
3 **Vicky** is very nice. I like ....
4 Karla's visiting **me and Trumpet**. She often visits ....
5 The **zoo** looks nice today. Let's take a photo of ....
6 **You and Patty** are hiding. I can't see ....

5 Read, choose and write. Then match.

I'm Polly Green. My brother Sam and (**1**) .....I..... are in the park today. Can you see (**2**) ....?
(**3**) ....'m on the swing. My doll is on the swing next to (**4**) ....
My brother is playing with a ball. (**5**) .... 's throwing (**6**) ....
Our dog is next to (**7**) .... It wants to play with the ball too. Mum and Dad are in the park with us. (**8**) ....'re sitting down on a bench. My bag is next to (**9**) ....
Dad is watching (**10**) .... and Mum is looking at (**11**) ....
(**12**) ....'s smiling.

1	(I)	Me
2	we	us
3	I	me
4	I	me
5	He	Him
6	it	them
7	he	him
8	They	We
9	they	them
10	we	us
11	he	him
12	She	Her

6 Answer about you.

1 When do you see your friends? .._I see them_.. every day / at weekends / on Saturdays.
2 When do you help your mum? ....
3 When does your grandma visit you? ....
4 When do you eat breakfast? ....
5 When does your best friend phone you? ....

1 Find and write.

```
d  a  n  c  e  l  p  m
i  s  t  f  z  n  l  e
v  i  w  e  a  r  n  e
e  n  i  s  i  r  y  t
p  g  n  r  z  x  p  z
o  n  g  c  e  z  q  s
a  w  d  l  a  u  g  h
```

1 Can I .....sing..... my new song for you?
2 I sometimes .... my friends in the park after school.
3 This is my favourite music! Let's ....
4 We always .... our armbands in the sea.
5 It's not funny. Don't ....
6 It's hot. Let's .... in the pool.

2 Read and tick (✓) or cross (✗).

1 This summer Tina will go to the mountains. She'll go climbing and she'll take lots of photos. She won't go to the beach.

 ✔  □  □

2 This summer Maria will go to the town. She'll go shopping and she'll buy some new clothes. She won't go diving.

 □  □  □

3 This summer Eddie will go to the forest. He'll go for walks and he'll look for animals. He won't go skiing.

 □  □  □

4 This summer Simon will go to the beach. He'll go diving and he'll play volleyball. He won't do homework.

 □  □  □

3 What will they be when they grow up?
Read, choose and write.

singer   ~~footballer~~
police officer   nurse
firefighter   zookeeper
photographer   reporter

1   Tom is good at sport.   He'll be a footballer.
2   We take great photos.   ....
3   Emma always helps people.   ....
4   I'm good at writing.   ....
5   Ben and Sam love music.   ....
6   You're very brave.   ....
7   My friend Mary loves animals. ....
8   Kevin wants to chase thieves. ....

4 What about you? Tick (✓) or cross (✗). Then write. Use 'll or won't.

When I grow up …

1   ....
2   ....
3   ....
4   ....
5   ....
6   ....
7   ....
8   ....
9   ....
10 ....

visit London
have a big house
be a reporter
drive a bus
go all around the world
go to school
be a firefighter
write books
help people
work in a library

5 Read and write 'll or won't.

1   Listen. The phone is ringing.   I 'll........ answer it.
2   Mum, we're hungry.   I .... cook some spaghetti.
3   It's cold.   I .... open the window.
4   I can't do my homework.   I .... help you.
5   Mum is tired. She's sleeping.   I .... be quiet. I .... play my drums.
6   I haven't got any money.   We .... go to the cinema. We .... go to the park.

Sally's Story
Our beautiful world

1 **Read and answer.**

1 Are the children throwing litter?
......Yes, they are.......

2 Is the woman's name Nina Nature?
....

3 Do the children make a wish?
....

4 Do they want to go to a zoo?
....

5 Is it cold and rainy in the desert?
....

6 Do they see camels in the desert?
....

7 Are the children climbing a mountain?
....

8 Do they see a whale in the ocean?
....

2 **Write the letters in the correct order. Then write the words.**

   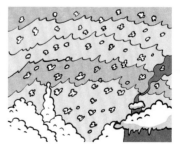

1 nunys

It's ....sunny........ .

2 dculyo

It's ....

3 yainr

It's ....

4 wosny

It's ....

3 Look and write.

1 Camels live in the ___desert.___
2 Parrots and monkeys live in the _____ .
3 Whales live in the _____ .
4 Bears live in the _____ .

4 Write in the correct order.

In the park …
1 play / football. / can / You
2 a bike. / You / ride / can
3 take / litter / must / You / home.
4 You / loud / music. / play / mustn't
5 climb / You / the trees. / mustn't

PARK RULES
1 You can play football.
2 _____
3 _____
4 _____
5 _____

What about you?

5 Read and tick (✓). Then write about the rules in your family.

I can …
watch TV in my bedroom.
play computer games.
play with my friends.
get up late on Sunday.

I must …
tidy my bedroom.
do my homework.
clean my teeth every day.
listen to my mum and dad.

I mustn't …
make a mess.
play loud music.
play basketball in my bedroom.
fight with my brother / sister.

RULES AT HOME
I can _____ and _____ .
I must _____ and _____ .
I mustn't _____ or _____ .

① **Choose and write.**

armbands   fisherman
flippers   bucket   spade
sandcastle   ~~sun~~   worried
boat   whale   far   near
people   swimsuit

The (**1**) ___sun___ is shining today but there aren't many (**2**) _____ at the beach.
There's a girl on the sand. She's wearing a (**3**) _____ . She's got a
(**4**) _____ and a (**5**) _____ . She's making a (**6**) _____ . There's a
man (**7**) _____ the girl. He's carrying (**8**) _____ . He wants to dive in the sea.
There's a boy in the sea. He's wearing (**9**) _____ . He isn't far from the beach. He isn't
swimming. There's a man in a (**10**) _____ . He's fishing. There's a (**11**) _____ in the
sea. The (**12**) _____ isn't (**13**) _____ because it's (**14**) _____ from the beach.

② **Write** can **or** can't.

Sam: It's John's birthday on Saturday. (**1**) ___Can___ I go to his party, please?
Dad: Yes, you (**2**) _____ . How old is he?
Sam: He's ten. (**3**) _____ I buy him a present?
Dad: Of course you (**4**) _____ .
Sam: Great! (**5**) _____ we go to the shops now?
Dad: No, I'm sorry, we (**6**) _____ . I'm working now. Let's go tomorrow.

③ **Write. Use** can, must **or** mustn't.

~~go for a walk~~   drink lots of water   go far from your friends   see lots of animals
take a map   throw litter

In the mountains
1 ___You can go for a walk.___
2 _____
3 _____
4 _____
5 _____
6 _____

4 Choose and write.

~~I~~ / me   you   you   He / him   She / her   it   they / them

Mary: Hi, Sue. (**1**) ___I___ 'm bored!

Sue: Do you want to come home with (**2**) _____ and watch TV?

Mary: Yes, please.

Sue: Hi, Mum. This is Mary. (**3**) _____ 's my friend. I sit next to (**4**) _____ at school.

Mum: Nice to meet (**5**) _____ , Mary.

Tom: Mum, where's my football? I can't find (**6**) _____ .

Sue: That's Tom. (**7**) _____ 's my brother. I like (**8**) _____ .

Dad: These football boots are for (**9**) _____ , Tom. Happy Birthday!

Tom: Thanks, Dad, (**10**) _____ 're great. Can I wear (**11**) _____ today?

5 Read, choose and write.

Dear Emma,

How are you? I'm very excited about my summer holiday. It (**1**) ___will___ be great! My family and I usually (**2**) _____ my cousins in July but we won't visit (**3**) _____ this summer.

We (**4**) _____ to the beach.

I (**5**) _____ diving lessons. I've got a new swimsuit, but I (**6**) _____ new flippers. I'll use my brother's flippers. He's very good at diving. Here's a photo of (**7**) _____ under the water.

We (**8**) _____ home in August. See you soon!

Love, Katie

1	(will)	won't	is being
2	visit	are visiting	will visit
3	they	their	them
4	'll go	go	went
5	have	had	'll have
6	won't buy	don't buy	will buy
7	her	he	him
8	came	'll come	comes

My English

Read and colour.

1   Can I go swimming, please? Yes, you can. / No, you can't.

2   You must be quiet in a library.

3   Look at Rob. Can you see him?

4   I'll be a firefighter when I grow up.

FUN TIME 3

1 **Say and circle the odd one out.**

1 bread	(drums)	umbrella	brown
2 train	crab	sun cream	crayon
3 grapes	playground	hungry	toothbrush
4 drink	children	zebra	dress
5 cry	train	treehouse	trumpet
6 brother	library	brave	photographer

2 **Write.**

1 first	**second**	**third**	fourth
2 June	July	August	
3 fourteen	**fifteen**	**sixteen**	
4 *Sunday*	*Monday*	*Tuesday*	
5 spring	summer	autumn	
6 fifty	**sixty**	**seventy**	

3 **Put a tick (✓) or a cross (✗) in the correct box and complete.**

		Yes	No
1	Pandas eat leaves.	✔ t	☐ a
2	It never snows in summer.	☐ e	☐ v
3	Mice are bigger than cats.	☐ n	☐ a
4	We'll go to school in the holiday.	☐ i	☐ c
5	Zebras are from China.	☐ m	☐ h
6	Reporters work for newspapers.	☐ e	☐ l
7	We must draw on our desks.	☐ s	☐ r

1 2 3 4 5 6 7

We must listen to our   t _ _ _ _ _ _

4 Write the questions. Then match.

1	2	3	4	5	6	7
please	have	got	yesterday	an	Can	you
8	**9**	**10**	**11**	**12**	**13**	**14**
on	watch	I	Do	Have	to	apple
15	**16**	**17**	**18**	**19**	**20**	**21**
Did	go	Is	tennis	Was	school	now
22	**23**	**24**	**25**	**26**	**27**	**28**
playing	happy	camera	TV	a	she	Sunday

1 6 / 10 / 2 / 5 / 14 / 1?
   Can I have an apple please?

2 11 / 7 / 9 / 25 / 8 / 28?

3 17 / 27 / 22 / 18 / 21?

4 15 / 7 / 16 / 13 / 20 / 4?

5 19 / 27 / 23 / 8 / 28?

6 12 / 7 / 3 / 26 / 24?

a Yes, she was.

b Yes, I did.

c No, you can't.

d No, she isn't.

e No, I haven't.

f Yes, I do.

5 Do the crossword and answer the question.

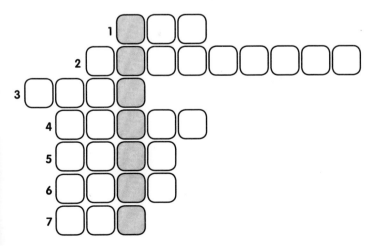

1 Dad is washing the car. Let's help
   ....

2 It .... rains in spring.

3 The boys .... have a great
   time at the party next weekend.

4 Did they .... their juice?

5 We .... a sandcastle at the
   beach yesterday.

6 My grandma is older ....
   my mum.

7 There aren't .... biscuits on
   the table.

Where will you go on ....? ....

Pearson Education Limited
Edinburgh Gate
Harlow
Essex CM20 2JE
England
and Associated Companies throughout the world.

www.pearsonelt.com

© Pearson Education Limited 2011

The right of Jeanne Perrett and Charlotte Covill and Tamzin Thompson to be identified as
authors of this Work has been asserted by them in accordance with the Copyright, Designs
and Patents Act 1988.

First published 2011
Twentieth impression 2020

ISBN: 978-1-4082-4975-8

Set in VagRounded Infant

Printed in Slovakia by Neografia

Acknowledgements
The publisher would like to thank the following for their kind permission to reproduce their
photographs:

(Key: b-bottom; c-centre; l-left; r-right; t-top)

Alamy Images: David Fleetham 64, Jon Arnold Images Ltd 76/5, William Leaman 62bl,
Nigel Reed QEDimages 76/4, Clive Sawyer 76/7, Neil Setchfield 76/2; **Trevor Clifford:** 43l,
87; **Corbis:** Bettmann 62tl, DLILLC 62bc, Tony Roberts 76/3; **Fotolia.com:** Vladimir Wrangel
62tr; **Getty Images:** Popperfoto 62tc; **Pearson Education Ltd:** Josephina Svania 5, 43r;
Rex Features: Jonathan Hordle 77, Ray Tang 76/6; **Thinkstock:** iStockphoto 62br

All other images © Pearson Education

Every effort has been made to trace the copyright holders and we apologise in advance
for any unintentional omissions. We would be pleased to insert the appropriate
acknowledgement in any subsequent edition of this publication.

Illustrated by Katerina Chrysohoou; GS Animation/Grupa Smacznego; HL Studios; Victor
Moschopoulos/chickenworks; Zaharias Papadopoulos/eyescream; Pedro Penizzotto/
Beehive; Christos Skaltsas/eyescream